# To Forget With Grace

## A poetic tale of living with early onset dementia

### Jacqui Peedell
### Jo Davies

# To Forget With Grace

## A poetic tale of living with early onset dementia

### Jacqui Peedell
### Jo Davies

*Chipmunkaclassic*

Published 2017
by Chipmunkaclassic

Published by
Chipmunka Classics
United Kingdom

http://www.chipmunkaclassics.co.uk

ISBN        9781783823444

Supported using public funding by
**ARTS COUNCIL ENGLAND**
LOTTERY FUNDED

Typeset in Kite One and Special Elite

# Contents

# About Us

**Jacqui Peedell** (on the right)

I am a Mosaic Artist. I was finally diagnosed with subcortical vascular dementia in 2014 but have had symptoms for 6 or 7 years. I have a daughter, Ruth, and live in Oxfordshire.

**Jo Davies** (on the left)

I am a One to One Support Worker for Young Dementia UK and have written poetry since I was seven.

# The Writing Process

Both Jacqui and Jo were keen to enlighten the public about the realities of living with Early Onset Dementia. Not in a gloomy way, but to inspire and maybe even raise a smile. So we hit upon the idea of a re-telling of Jacqui's story as a series of illustrated poems: her story with its vibrant background, its bravery, and her never-failing pragmatism in the face of life's ups and downs.

So thanks to a grant won from The Rain Maker Network by our friend Larry Gardiner, we were able to spend several winter evenings working together on this project. We began the writing process by thinking of several titles that meant something to Jacqui, then during the next few weeks we focused on one or two titles per session. Jacqui talked and Jo wrote.

Once home with the gathered material, Jo sculpted each monologue into poetry, cherry-picking from the richness of Jacqui's dialogue. Then, together, Jo and Jacqui fleshed out the work until the piece succeeded in saying what Jacqui had intended. The final stage was to link each poem with an image.

It was a very creative and cathartic time.

We - Jacqui and Jo - are grateful to Young Dementia UK and to The Rain Maker Network for enabling us to collaborate on this project, to Cathy Hattam Photography for the pictures of us at work and play, to OpenStreetMap for the map on pages 53 and 54 (it is © OpenStreetMap contributors), to Dave Favis-Mortlock for all his amazing help with the editing, and to Chipmunka for publishing the finished product.

We hope you enjoy it.

# Prologue

## To Forget with Grace

The ability to forget with grace.

Grateful, glad, grace.
Remembering, rising, rage, regrets, romance
Acute, ambled, able, anxious
Creativity, comfort
Energy, eager.


Anxious, I spend days trying to think of all the ingredients I need in order to make an act happen. So I work in circles that then become numbers or boxes. I start from the end and work my way back to the start. For the things I have to tackle everyday, sometimes common sense is not there for me.

All sorts of things happen - from struggling with technology to getting locked in changing rooms or struggling with understanding how to get in and out of certain types of clothes.

I am the sort of person who can make macaroni cheese and forget the cheese.

Sometimes I find cups of coffee in the microwave two days later.

I tell myself all the different things I need to do in the next hour and then, in what seems like the next minute, I find myself on a train doing something totally different.

That is why, when I make my mosaic - it is the one thing I can do and be amazed by the end result. It is the one thing that I am totally in control of... It is my liberation... my sanctuary...

The mosaic is often not planned - it is a free flowing creative process.

## Mask

I made the mask and realised it was a self portrait.
The irregularity of the yellow and orange signifies the random connections that were being made in my brain.
The beaded areas signify the pain.
The spiral of the eye signifies the chaos in which I see things and the depth of thinking I need -
in order to fully comprehend situations.
However my eyes see different things,
one eye sees chaos and randomness,
the other protrudes and keeps things grounded
in order for me make the chaos stand still -
and to put things in perspective.

The spirals on my cheeks represent the acute pain I was having with my teeth - which were falling out one by one due to the medication I was given.

My mouth represents my truth and my ongoing ability to speak the best that I can. And the blues represent the love I have for most things that I see.

This process gives me a sense of order - but the elements of that order are hard for me to envisage; I can only see the finished picture - but how I get there - I am not sure - but it is my strong belief that the universe can guide me. And for as long as I can, I hope I can trust in this, without the darker side appearing along with thoughts of abandonment - both of them and you.

And trusting that today will not be one of those random days when no matter how hard I try, I find it impossible, both through lack of energy and knowledge to complete the simplest of tasks.

I want to be on my own - frustrated and sad. I want to hide away and be insular, not because I am depressed but because I don't want people to see how confused I seem. Because if they do see me on a bad day - they judge me from that and suddenly I find they are telling me that I can't do things and then suddenly things are taken away, and when things are taken away they get lost. Things disappear from my life. I find myself robbed - my time is being stolen.

You question me and I am blank. You ask me and I lie. You speak to me and I am silent. I walk away - because you don't have the time to hear my answer.

I am misunderstood.

But where there is loss there are also many things to be gained.
Life might be limited and present itself in a different way but it is still
fulfilling.

It's important **not** to put **emphasis** on *fear* - but to think of the
nicest things that could happen. To use the brain creatively to think
round problems or trials and make new pathways and connections.
Allowing myself to to be....
.....Accepting the moment and letting time pass...
............not seeing this as an end but a beginning...

## The Making of the Mask

Liberation, sanctuary, free flowing process,
giving visual and sensual perspectives on
What I see in life.
Signifying pain and suffering,
confusion
The search for a sense of balance
positivity
Trying to find sense in disorder.
Being held together
brought together
gelled together
by those certain strands that help me
to speak my truth in a way that defines me now
(A far cry from who I was).

## Morning

Open eyes
pain
back
shoulders
lie
stretch
hip stuck
no swinging legs
slow motion get out
kettle
pee
coffee
9 medical miracles
Every morning
all preventatives
4 for diabetes
1 blood pressure
1 cholesterol
1 for weeing
1 for anti fits
1 for dementia.

I have a tune
rehearsing
rewinding
repeating
the chant
needle to grove

Aricept yellow
Oxybutynin blue
Simvastatin red
colour codes for safety
1
1
2
1
1
2
over and over
again.

And then
The pharmacist changes
the box from blue to green
from diamonds to squares
remodelling- remoulding
so I don't know
which is which
disturbing my rhythm
wrecking my routine
confusing me.
The drugs are a trial
but I am no monkey
and
I choke on rocks.
I'm not a pill popper
and they wont go down
then I get down
and tears.

## Lunchtime

I like to eat out some times
I go alone
I heard they do good burgers
in the Auctioneer
so
decided I would
take a trip –
hot food dream
hunger pangs
idea makes
rare juices run
yum –
jump in car
remind myself
when I get there
I am going to order a burger –
so I drive down the road
indicate
look left and right
tell myself
gonna get a burger.

Go round the roundabout
stop at the zebra crossing
check the speed limit
tell myself
you're gonna get a burger
stop at the lights
check the mirror

signal
manoeuvre
click click
gonna get a burger
get to the pub
climb out of the car
quick step along the path
yes going to get a burger
walked in
everybody moving
people
music
find a nice table
sit
still going to get a burger.

Order drink
JO2
wrong name
means oxygen
I remember that way.
OK burger
handed menu
words drift
blank and busy
dyslexically blind
have to guess what is there.
But I can't find a burger
I know they have burgers
nonsense eyes
don't ask

panicking
where's the bloody burger?
Letters spin
illiterate
waiter turns up
"What would I like?"

Brain daze
nothing there
empty
....what do I want ?
I might have said enchilada
or dough bread
the mystery is mine.
In front of me
sits
triangles of soft – floury –
thick white uncooked pastry
stuffed with cold white slimy mozzarella
and beefy tomato.
My allergic dream.
I eat everything
just like that
And my irritated bowel screams.
What about the burger?

Stomach so swollen
writhing pain
so bad I can't press
the pedals
to drive home.

## Evening

is
tea time
with food as a 'GOT TO'
drug swallowing makes it a necessity
and it's usually too late
after a hard day doing nothing
(that I can remember)
to make much.
I pick at peanuts and raisins
and if I can get away with it,
I won't eat.

I watch NCIS or CSI
every night
it makes me feel good.
All the characters are my friends-
Gil Grissom – Jim Brass – Nick Stokes
comfortingly familiar.
Must have seen each program 100 times
and to test my memory
I like to try and remember the story line.
These episodes are
ear buddies
I watch TV with my ears
because I am always doing things
but what I'm doing
I don't know.
In between 10 and 12 pm,
I plan for the next day.

I have to try and
look at the weather
plan my clothes
try and visualise myself
doing the thing I need to be doing
so that when I do the thing - it's not so strange
because I've already done it in my head-
because I am paranoid
that if I can forget what I did today,
then I will forget what I need to
be doing tomorrow.
I think about tomorrow
but I don't go further than that
because just to do tomorrow
is hard work

I can't amble through life
like I could when I was normal -
the more precise I can be
about what it is I need to do,
the better it is
because
I don't like spanners in the works
I don't like surprises.
I Google everything
so I can get a real picture up, of what it's like
before I go there.
And with people
I have to anticipate
their mood, their reaction, their intention
I have to know

I have to absorb
I have to put everything in its place
so that I have an answer ready
so that I give the right reaction
so that I say the right thing.

At some point
I go outside
Always - snow or rain.
I listen to my inner alarm clock
and wander to the bottom of the garden
and walk along the zig zag
and around the car park and
I look at the moon and say thank you for
all the good things that have happened -
then when I come in
I feel calm.
I need to be calm
because the night frustrates and
I know I won't sleep.
A glug of bedtime mirtazapine
quick nodding off
sleep for two hours
then awake
till 6.00 -
never thinking about anything,
in a semi stupor,
watching stars,
rather than counting sheep.

## The Zone

Daytime
most days I have
a zone when nothing happens
nothing moves an inch
total stillness
a sundowner -
apparently these things
can happen with dementia.

Nothing stirring in my brain
no colour
no sound
no feeling
a black hole
in my universe of grey matter -
as if there is an overload
and then a total shut down.

I can look at the clock and it was 4
and then **ping** it's 7...

## Music

energises
the mind
the body
you can bop
and chill.
I love it
I will listen to anything
every kind up to classical –
give me Tchaikovsky on a Sunday morning and
I don't apologise to my neighbours
when I turn it up –
It **GROUNDS** me.

Music doesn't make me reminisce much –
but I might get a sensation
of remembering –
Dirty Dancing
and Michelle
setting me up on a date
with a sweaty little man
getting me drunk
and inevitability –
but all I remember is
I hurled him off –
his salty beads rolling
down on me–
Michelle was **for** it.
**DETERMINED** –

21

I was **against** it
No Thanks...
and
it all went wrong -
but I remember dancing in this huge kitchen
to the Dirty Dancing theme tune
      **Happy**.

I love Latino
and reggaeton -
rude licks,
lyrics you shouldn't be proud of
but make you shake
all your bits.
It works
and its been a long time since I felt **sexy**-
I don't even know if I know how to be sexy
but if that track came on
I know I would
move my bum
my boobs
and jive.

Music makes me move
I love to move
I may make a fool of myself
in a room full of statues
but
at least I show
I know the music -
I love the music

*it is pure expression.*

*You can't dance to*
*an aria in opera -*
*it's all in your head*
*you can't dance*
*it ain't the same.*

*The last time I went to a club*
*its all about the bass*
*no treble -*
*all this DJ scratch*
*using old stuff mixed with new*
*it's manufactured*
*it's packaged*
*like a ready meal from Tesco -*
*plastic music for a sleepy mind.*

*I like*
*real*
*raw*
*passionate*
*music -*
*hand-carved*
*original.*

*It doesn't matter if you're with a child*
*an old man -*
*even a dog...*
*you can open yourself up -*

solid stuff from the past
penned and ink-stained in
authenticity.

Al Green...
'All my love',
tuneful, melodic and it's got rhythm -
expressing itself so well
you can express yourself.
He sings "...What is time? ... It goes by so slowly
but time can do so much...".

It doesn't matter who sings those words
it evokes such a lot
it is timeless
ageless
enduring.

Once said
it can't be unsung.

# Food

## (Essentially a Dementiary Tale)

Although my stomach is rumbling
Although I feel uncomfortable
Although it's 8 o'clock at night
I still don't realise
that these signs
mean I am hungry.
I might even say the words "It's dinner time"
but it doesn't mean anything -
so wondering
about my path -
knowing something is missing
and that I am searching,
I light an incense stick-
and strangely
with this one sense awoken
the fragrance will alert me
to the knowledge that I am hungry -
maybe it nudges my taste buds
into life...

Smell can have so many memories
and feelings attached to it-
so much of the past
not far off- like a whisper.

Quite often when I am confused,
I light incense because it reminds me to think about
what what I need to think about.
My mind tells me
to just
stop
sit down and usually
there is a realisation.

It could be that I ran a bath two hours ago
and it might tell me that I need to be in that bath
I may go to the loo and look at the
full bath, -
see the steam rising...
and it still doesn't mean anything-
It just doesn't register.

I may return an hour later-
the water is lukewarm
and on the next visit it is cold.

I see the cold water
it sits there for two or three days
and eventually the penny drops.

Smell to me
    means cleanliness -
        I am comforted.

# Apples

I know that I like an apple.
I regularly go to the supermarket and buy a bag.

They look crisp and fresh
rosy and healthy
I imagine crunching and eating
biting delight-
definitely good for me-
but when I buy apples
Then return home-
I place them carefully in a bowl
and I look at them
but I do not slaver
at the thought of eating them,
my mouth does not water.

There is a detachment between
the idea and the reality.

Days after days go by
and I look at those apples
a week will pass
a month will pass
and I will not have taken a single bite
and as they are not eaten
they shrivel
grow old
become dull
unattractive.

I know the bin calls
I look at them
And minutes may pass.

I know
they are compost.

But at the final point
just before I throw them away
I take one and place it on the chopping board
and I find a knife and slice it in half.

I stare and stare - white pulp and pips
and maybe I could take a piece
but I simply have
no idea what to do.

It couldn't be more obvious.
But I don't eat it...

That's why I eat banana
you can peel and bite a banana
it's easy
it's sweet
it's dense
it's filling
a banana makes you go
**zzzzzzOsh**
and gives you energy.

## Stew

I enthusiastically made a beef stew.
Ingredients:
- **beef**
- **carrots**
- **onions**
- **swede**
- **stock**
- **herbs.**

I spent time preparing
and making it right
I enjoyed the smell
of the meat browning off
and the veg browning off
I got it in the oven.
Slow cooked
with three hours passing.
I knew it smelt nice
I took it out
took the lid off
and saw the herbs on the top.

I just stood staring at it
although it looked delicious
the thought of eating it was so complicated
so nonsensical
that I covered it back up
and left it for another hour.

It was really late....
10 o'clock
I know I felt hungry
I could still smell it
I went back
and looked at it again.

I like carrots
I took a carrot off the top
once I tasted it
my stomach kicked in and said
**Bingo!**
This is what we want
but I could only have a small bowl.

I don't know how long this takes
I don't  do these things properly
I don't do time.

# Can I Still Wonder?

I still like to ponder
and mull
maybe it is on a tangent
but sometimes I think deeply on a
topic of the day -
I bite the bullet -
And find a hundred different things about the subject.
My mind wanders down unknown paths
I can get lost... blank.... empty
and I might forget what the topic of the day was
but at least I was trying.

And when I have space - I can do it
but when I haven't got space, I can't do it
and nothing gets done.

When I am on my own I have the opportunity
to see
if I can do those things.

In my brain I think I can
but in reality
perhaps I can't.

## Flow

This is what I think -
my philosophy
is not rigid
once you have your own mind
you must be flexible
because everything changes.
My philosophy has always been
that whatever it is you want to do
you can do.
I don't believe
if your disabled
or depressed
or poor
it changes anything -
nothing is out of reach.
Always have goals
no matter how small or how big -
we are only on this earth plain
one time -
no matter what you believe
anyone on this earth at this moment
is only living this moment
once.

Live this life
as it is
now.

And even though
I am not a Christian,
the Ten Commandments
are a good staple for morals -
so have high morals
but not so much that you can't enjoy yourself
and you become gaoled by them -
If morals were rigid, we would not have scientists,
physicists, astronauts... we would not explore.

Life is about growth
and not constraint.
so maybe what I'm trying to do is grow my brain -
If the average person uses only 10 per cent of their brain -
well I am planning to access the other 90 per cent of mine!
I am learning
learning all the time.

Some things I do seem to get better and better -
but that goes against the dementia -
because having dementia
should mean I am being diminished.
I am mindful of everything I do
(my dementia forces me to be)
and surely this means
I am keeping my brain
alive
and making new pathways.

I try and be still
let quiet moments pass

allow time for thoughts
to appear and direct my actions –
I try never to get into a spin.

I ask the universe
"Please give me the answer"
all the answers to every epidemic
illness
stupidity
greed
fear.

And the answers lie here
before us
on this earth
and above.

Yet we don't see answers easily
we don't slow down –
we are dazzled by computers
the internet and TV –
all the answers are there
but we don't know how to look.

I feel stuff
I keep open –
a buzzing mass of DNA
making my shape.

Everyone can hone in if they want
but you have to be open,
unafraid,
selfless.
You have to understand
you are an atom
and when atoms get together
they make things.

I am part of you –
you are part of me.

A cup is solid matter
a tree is living matter –
if it's not plastic or china
it is living and breathing –
and because we live and breathe,
we can pass through each other.
We are one organism
a collective
an energy.
We are never truly alone.

As a race
we feel superior
but we are so dazzled by
our own existence that
if there was another energy
we wouldn't see it
but just because

we don't see it
doesn't mean
it isn't there.
I believe in Karma
no barriers
or boundaries -
I used to have brick walls to the ceiling,
heart blocked in,
arms folded,
**keep away,**
not interested -
then I started
to learn to be open.

I went into the library
(something drew me in)
I found myself in front of
a book called
'Breath' -
I thought, "What the hell are you holding that for?"
"You don't read..."
then I thought
"You've got it in your hand -
you may as well take it".

## Controller

What was it I wanted?

I knew I didn't want to put the TV on.
I had to tell myself
**YOU ARE NOT PUTTING THAT TV ON**
And I know there's something else I want.
But what?

There were three remotes on the table-
They all said Sony -
I had a go with each one to see what they did
and I accidentally put the music on-
the player was hidden under stuff.
I saw Cafe del Mar appear
in digital red letters
on a black box-
and calming music began
breathing into the space-
calming and cool
but what had happened?

I hadn't figured it out
but the music came
like a miracle
and I sat there
and there was nobody
and I was in the music
and I was drifting with the music
and the music filled me.

It
takes the edges off
and softens me.

# Friendship

Friendship is
somebody that you know,
that you love, that you trust
even if they're not there,
in the same space,
in the same room,
and it is a comfort.

We may not speak for weeks
but you know me so deeply
that we have
telepathic communication
a sixth sense
growing intuition.
We know what smells one another like
what tastes
what colours.
You can be in Essex
and I can be here -
120 miles west and
we can shop and come
back with identical clothes.

I know when I can have a deep
relationship with someone
within five minutes

of meeting them -
I ask a certain question
and expect to hear a selfless answer -
I ask them something else and expect a humble answer -
and another and expect self belief -
and another and expect loyalty.
I want to see if they have true qualities-
compassion, honesty, empathy.
If they can show a little of those three
then there is something to build on
but these days I forget to contact a friend newly made,
and with that goes the opportunity.

A friend is somebody who will
walk through many traumas with you -
and you with them -
side by side
without judgement
and when disagreements arrive
we disagree without anger
staying strong in our own opinions
and belief
and yet still being accepted
and loved.

We learn and feed from one another
We grow and harvest with one another
revealing faults and weaknesses

and accepting them with humour.
And we can laugh and kick one another under the table
when we get things wrong.

We are one another's defenders
we protect the precious bubble
with a heavily woven tapestry
of shared memories
and stand shoulder to shoulder
when under attack.
We adapt and change
to circumstance—
chameleon-like
we move from
criticism to compassion.
We talk openly
never thinking about what we may
say...
...words fly
like butterflies free to drift anywhere
and when
I am tired and low
and find myself in darkness
friendship is the light.

Friendship
from root to tip -
sharing our truth.

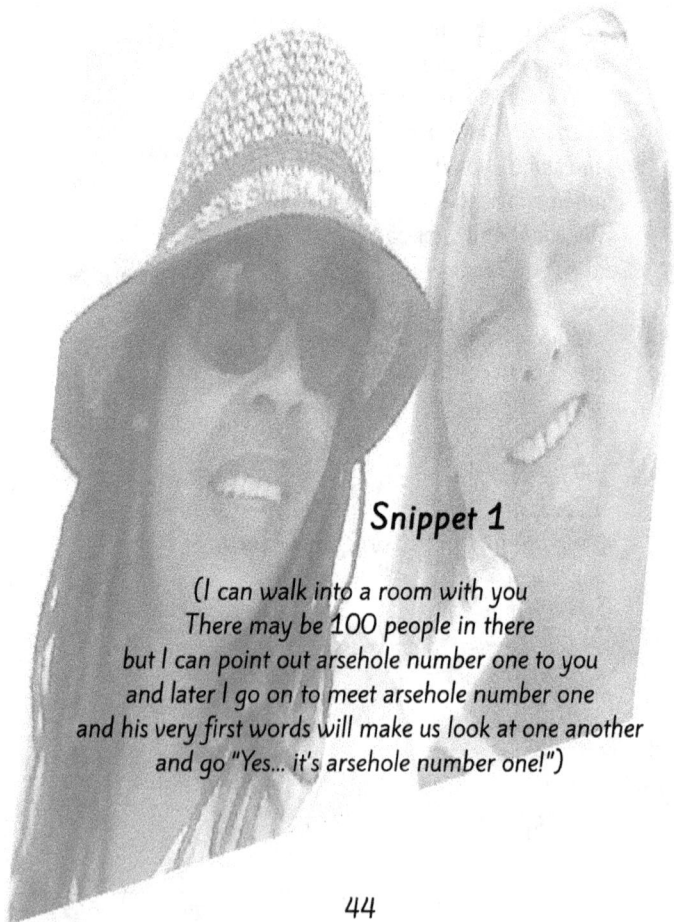

## Snippet 1

(I can walk into a room with you
There may be 100 people in there
but I can point out arsehole number one to you
and later I go on to meet arsehole number one
and his very first words will make us look at one another
and go "Yes... it's arsehole number one!")

## Stroke

Dementia creeps
    along my nerve endings
soft head headache
    depressing scalp
skull bone fluff and feather
fluid **whoosh**
    in ear drum
a cacophony
of debilitation.
A hit smack bang
and dizzy spinning of plates
thoughts in a maze
    set brain-fire burning
    and
      synapse sizzle
      to dull quiet
        then shut down.

Magnificent living tree
    felled
      by
      a
    single
    stroke.

# Checkpoints

(The chain of events
that I pre-arrange
drive me forward-
I move from one check point to another.)

I park in the Auctioneer
but I only ever walk in a straight line
I never go off to the sides
little streets won't tempt me.

So out of car and:
*1<sup>st</sup> checkpoint.*

Cancer Research is on the right
*2<sup>nd</sup> checkpoint*
glance at Barnardo's  on the left
go urgh
just can't go in there.
Smell.

The market (bottom of street) is my
*3<sup>rd</sup> checkpoint*
walk through
"...pawnd of bananas"
and the meat guy yelling.

Then stop at the drunk man
hiccup and snoring -

and pass by the first flowers
Mrs Bouquet
and if I go into the Quay
I know I am
going to the toilet.

## Checkpoint 4
Cut through to Caffé Nero
smell the coffee.

## Checkpoint 5
down to Wilkinson's
and to Katherine House
I have to go there
even if it's just to stand outside
the window—
even if it's closed
I have to walk that extra 100 yards
just to get there.

## Checkpoint 6
past the spud man
and I think
"I hope you're selling spuds"
but he never does.

I don't know how he survives -
always say a little prayer for the spud man.

## Checkpoint 7
second flower man at Barclays
wish they could get more creative:
    funerals
    weddings
    birthdays
    more funerals.

## Checkpoint 8
books zone but I don't know the name
but Shoes Zone's on the corner
I go in...

## Checkpoint 9
cross the road
Macall's newsagents
skinny little shop
maybe baccy.

## Checkpoint 10
through alleyway
head up Parson's street again
Barnardo's on the right
Cancer Research on the left
back to the Auctioneer.

Before a journey
I always study this map in my mind
re planned, re-examined,
gone over.

I tell myself all the things
I am going to see
I rehearse the route
I have to be super dooper observant
compared to most people -
I'm constantly checking in -
so that if something isn't there
or different
or moved
I can reorientate myself -
I can feel the difference
So I notice it.

## Shopping

How did I end up in a supermarket?
When my whole day has been planned,
no trips out,
just mosaic jewellery to create.
I had been feeling peckish,
checked the clock,
time for lunch -
OK can deal with that.
Phone rings
long chat with friend,
next known action
I am battling for breath and space in a car park
trolley bashing in an overcrowded supermarket.
(it is probably five years since I have done a Saturday shop).

I persist and do my shopping
but my mind is saying "This is all wrong".

Finally I return home
some two and a half hours later,
Only to discover I have already done the shopping.

I have no room
for another twelve yogurts,
a week's selection of cheese,
and even the freezer groans as it cannot take
another packet of fish fingers,
assorted meats, or a bag of frozen peas.

# Tricks for Dementia

## Ticking Boxes (Travelling Trick)

Ignition ignited.
I come out of here
I go to the middle bend
and to the next bend
I drive up the hill
and find myself at the T-junction
I turn left.
All these initial boxes have to be ticked.
Then roundabout 1
roundabout 2
past Ruth's work-
then the Police Station.
I have to say to myself
I have a short rat run
I have to keep on track.
If something unexpected
happens I can be completely thrown
I turn into blubbering jelly
and if I lose my way
A policeman may help.
Once in London
on public transport
a strange bus
(the Oxford Tube to Victoria-
I knew where I was)
but National Express took me to an

unfamiliar end of
Victoria bus station
and I was lost
but what I did was follow the crowd,
I just kept following the people
praying that they were going to the train station-
some trailed off but I followed those pulling
suitcases... that's where they were going.
I stand and look
back against a building
and I watch
a man with a badge and a waistcoat
I don't know what he is called
or who he is -
I walk past him trying to read his name badge
I walk past again
and eventually I ask him
"What are you doing here?"
all blunt and attitude
and he says "I am here to help".
so I say "Please help me".

I'm not afraid to approach people
I don't worry about what I say
I just say anything -
And if I'm out of my depth
I blabber -
that's why I am a home girl.
Because if I have a shock
I wet myself.

## Tricks with My Clothes

I only buy certain types of things-
  shoes with lots of laces
   but with a trick of a zip at the side
   because I can't do laces up any more.

      I like clothes that look complicated
      but where there is a secret
       like velcro or a tie-
        I don't do zips at the back-
         stretchy sports bras work
          so I don't have to worry about the clasps-
           pull it on - pull it off
            and I just slide it down my legs
             the long-distance route.
              I leave my clothes inside out
               so when I put them on
                they go on the correct way
                 but it doesn't always work
                  upside down - back to front
                  because
                   when things are the right way round
                   it totally throws me
                    I just cant put it on -
                    once I got stuck in my jumper
                   half in - half out
                  waiting for rescue.

On my own-
I wear easy stuff,
jogging bottoms
and tee shirts
but if I have a visitor
I will put my glad rags on
and if I buy something that I like
and it is comfortable
and the sales are on
invariably I will buy another the same
stick to what I know
just buy a different colour.
When I go out with regular people
I try and do what I do
and look the norm-
but in my head I'm counting
on them -
I'm blasé in my way
If they lead me
I don't have to do any
thinking.

## Squash Trick

I make one full glass of squash in the morning
I sip and swallow my pills so there is two-thirds left.
Then at lunch time I see I have one glass, two-thirds full
 of squash in front of me.
  Everything else is clear, no mess -
   just the glass prominent on the table-
    then I know that after lunch I have to take my next pills
    and I have one-third left
    and then at supper
     I see that that one-third of a glass of squash
     and I know that I have to take my bedtime pills.
     It is sacred..
      a ritual....
       a life saver....
       that one
        glass
        of squash.

## Smell Trick

I use smell as a trick -
last night I put Patchouli oil in my hair.
I like the smell of Patchouli.

I put it in
so that the whiff
would kick-start the memory
and
the requirement
that I need to dye my hair
otherwise I would forget.

# Surroundings

When I was OK
I worked as an interior designer
I was very specific -
precise -
I knew if something needed moving
half an inch
or a tiny adjustment was necessary
to colour or shade.
When I lived at home with my parents,
I didn't notice my surroundings
familiarity made me blind.
Though I knew they were grandiose
in their taste...
compared to others.

Before this
brain dying
I was very eclectic - now I am simplistic,
before I was tastefully cluttered,
now I am clean, serene and uncomplicated.

In Spain
we lived high on a mountain
in a ruin with a roof
pure candour
raw air
unadulterated,
but now I need comfort.
I don't need to have what the neighbours have

I like arm chairs
Queen Anne chairs
beautiful chairs
I like tables
plaster work
texture
I understand that Art Deco
can live next to Shaker
neighbours in harmony.

I love explosions of colour
I am a complete fanatic-
I dream of walls covered in hot burnt orange
and blue Arabic glow.

But...
because of my dementia
I need calm,
my walls are green and
green is the colour of love,
whist I am not an infant
who seeks a gentle lullaby in powder pink or
baby blue - I seek comfort in this verdant wash.

My room for sitting
reveals obvious prompts
to glare at me
with hopeful eyes
demanding action.
Books
DVDs

CDs
for behind closed doors they would remain
unseen... forgotten.
I fill my walls with reminders.

I like reminders:
A framed ivory Buddha head from my sister
(the best thing she gave me- that I truly liked)
two flowery hair bands from a riverside festival
bought for my birthday on a day full of summer
one for me.... one for my daughter.

The gold and grey bowl
with a mosaic secret
spread wide inside
crammed with the blues and greens
of the Mediterranean.

The pottery Grecian urn
curved with ancient
shades of clay,
matt greens and browns
set like stone.

Art Deco glass frog
melted like a child's boiled sweet
(had it for a hundred years)
knick-knacks - ornaments - charms
always travelled with me
across countries
and seas.

Small heart matching the frog,
green for love and calm.

Rosaries of Ruth
mother to daughter
tangled and uneven
like us
unbalanced and off- centre
but gradually re-arranged
and gathering new symmetry.

Reflection - texture - feeling -
China crown prince sitting
quietly in a corner
to be mosaiced -
an artistic metamorphosis
into a king.

A delicately painted Chinese pot from Hong Kong
sitting beside European swag
A reluctant mix of east with west
meeting with Zen.

The umbers - the burgundy -
the smoky brown.

A tangerine candle
carved with the hand of Hamsa
to shine-
my symbol of protection
lit with the heady aroma of Morocco.

The collection of little Buddhas
one for health - one for wealth
one for happiness - one for grace -
beside the
red resin frog with a coin in his mouth
facing the window and door,
promising that money will always come.

I watch the objects
gaze at me
fixed
under the shade
late in the evening.

Reflections lift me
angels arising
out of the shadows
into leafy glades -
casting light on confusion,
offering guidance,
opening minds,
seeing things within things -
fizz of static
in the silence
unmoving -
feet firmly planted -
the green room earthing me in.

# Sparked Out

In Spain they gave me drugs that
the English doctors
didn't approve of -
they said
these were the kind of drugs
they give a
**Broadmoor patient.**

One day
I took my night time pills instead
of my day time pills
I was driving down the mountain
on my way to meet a client
whose house I was designing.
I drove down the mountain
screeching round the hair-pin bends
car on two wheels
hair flying
when I got to the bottom
I said
"You know what? I feel sleepy!"
And climbed into the back seat
and
**sparked out.**

# The Seasons

## Winter

In Spain
winter is the time to get logs in
but here
the clocks alter
misplace routine
another mess-up
nothing synchronised.

Rhythm changes
we lose ourselves
in later hours
my time my day
doesn't fit with other peoples' day
four or five hours behind
your tempo
snail slow.

I have dinner when you go to bed.

Robins
But no Christmas
can't relate
no Jesus - no crib - no three blokes
following stars.

Relying on TV
for glassy eyed entertainment-
then no escape,
super-glued to Dove and beauty oil-
relentless noisy advertising -
government supported,
while the little man
crushing almonds gets nothing.

Oh yes I need a Pop Tart.

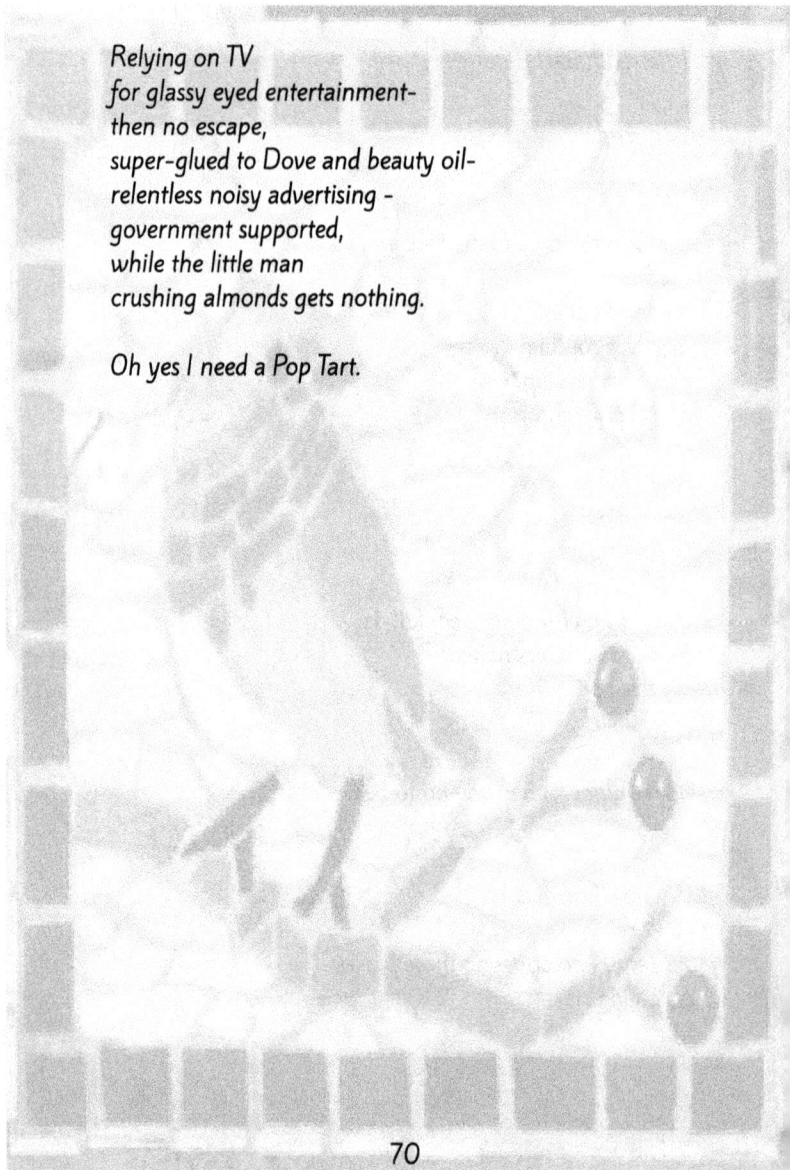

## Spring

Full of expectancy and
promising
the inevitability
of summer
light and warmth
green life unfurling
giving birth
blossoming
people smile
abundantly.

Spring to clean
house and eyes
polish vision
see anew
sales rife
consumer heaven
new clothes
new shoes
new skin.

First time to really breathe
in deep
explosion of pigmentation
and growth
waiting to see
what treasure
is revealed

and discover where
forgotten bulbs sprout.

Artists
crawl out of creative hibernation.

A visionary wake up
new aspirations alive
with the vibrancy of nature's
palette.

## Summer

Summer blue sky
balloons
brightness
and smiles
everybody happy
except the British
who moan about the heat.

Summer is adventure
a time to step
out of our comfort zone
new places new faces -
we indulge in our passions -
a time to breathe -
seaside
countryside
mountainside
bare foot
connecting
with the earth-
scrunching toes
into sand and grass
sucking up energy
everything creative abounds -
fine art appears in the most stagnant
of objects or beings.

In Spain it was so hot
there was nothing to do so

we used to watch the ants make paths
and watch the moss grow
in this fast lane of germination.
Summer is the best time to travel
because even the dullest buildings
look good in the sunshine.

Audrey Hepburn scarves
and fast cars
reliving the past
but enjoying the now
connected to everyone
and everything -
feeling every heart beat.

Summer is a blue dot
that bursts into prisms
of light and colour and movement.
Summer is the promise of youth.
A rejuvenation,
summer flowers reflected
in all the flowing cool clothes
people wear -
open air festivals,
concerts and music.

It's just a celebration really.

It should be never-ending.
Summer.

## Autumn

Browns
and yellows and orange
reds and blue and greys,
a change in the days
mist in the morning
and fog at night.
The closing-down sale of nature
and life.
Mowers are put to bed -
paddling pools
are in the shed
and all the summer flowers
are nearly dead.
Crisp smoky breath-
watching your own lively
vapour trail stretch out before you.
Cold and crunching
underfoot
usual chores
but a hat and gloves
and a brisk
wind around your ears.
And on that first autumn sunny day
everyone
flocks out
to try to breathe in
and hold on to
the last gasp
        of summer.

## Snippet 2

*If I can't remember someone*
*I don't worry my head about it*
*I just wait for them*
*to finish their conversation and say "Bye".*

## Snippet 3

*If you don't look like you have dementia*
*in other peoples' eyes you ain't got dementia.*
*They say they forget stuff too,*
*it's normal.*
*But it ain't that easy.*

## New Shoes

You see those shoes
sitting in a window?
70 quid -
imagine you own them
you have paid for them
believe you are wearing them
they are there in your cupboard
under your stairs
all you have to do is put your
attention and intention there
and those shoes will find your feet.

Plug your connectivity in
positive - negative like a battery.
Yes! - You always want the positive
if you say I can't - you won't.
Brain believes **You**
Brain is receptive
Brain is listening.

You say I can I can I can
you can sprout and blossom.

The universe does not work in
hours and minutes
the universe works in its own time -
(I no longer understand hours and minutes either)
but I know if I ask - it will come

maybe not today, tomorrow
next week... next month... but it will come.

I am a big believer
in manifestation.

Imagine a garden full of weeds
if you bend down and plant a seed
and pull the weeds out
and allow the seed to grow -
you will end up with a lovely flower garden -
everything in your brain that says "I can't" is a weed -
pull out those weeds and free yourself.

## Habit

Huge amounts of TV
for no bollocking reason
but conforming -
  sit here,
    coach potato,
      yawning
        into the stratosphere.

Null and void.

# Ruth

She's been glum
for a long time
its been
hard as her mum
because
I just want her to be happy-
but with the magazine
the revealing
and unravelling
the experience -
she strives to be more positive -
day by day
she makes
small
steps
one foot in front of the other.

A forward move
but to where?

But she knows with little steps
nothing bad will happen.

Her young eyes see she has a life
without me-
because we hold on too tight
and constrict one another-
but gradually
the glue un-sticks

and we climb away -
parting clouds
allow the sun to shine.

I want her to go
and be free of worry-
I want her to be light hearted
and to grow and flourish
and spring high
and dive into life

Because I too
need to dive into life -
to be confident enough
to make my own lunch,
get into a bath,
do the things I need to do.

It's a long time since I have been alone -
but aloneness propels me forward
into my time
my space
my routine.

A little bit more room for breathing
means tiny spears of light
entering the muddle of a day
incense
and a memory of meditation.

Peaceful

*thinking moments -*

*daily giving thanks -*
*deep conversation*
*with the celestial.*

*Small rituals*
*that mean help and*
*hope -*
*a sense of self -*
*though I have dementia*
*I am.*

*And in the manner*
*of all fledglings -*
*so Ruth will be.*

## Snippet 4

Dementia means if I watch a TV ad selling digestive biscuits
and they use a furry pussy cat leaping out of the packet as part of it -
I ask
"Are they expecting us to eat a cat?"

That totally throws me.

If they advertise a biscuit I expect to see a biscuit
not a cat.

I am literal like that.

## 'The Sun' Interview

They came
because of the film
'Still Alice'.
It's how it began
a real story about living with dementia
aged fifty three.

Two days on the phone
long times... many words
loud speaker
me and my daughter
the interview lady talking
chatting
a simple conversation -
and she would say a question like...
"Did you work?"
And I only said one job.
I couldn't remember any other
because as we race
there's no time for thinking
but later my friend reminded me -
I had re-designed three houses,
worked as a painter,
a gardener, a builder,
opened a bar
and worked within the community
amongst other things!
But only 'painter' came out.

*There is no time to think -*
*no break*
*no pause*
*no breath*
*and that was the first time I started to feel sad*
*when I was being interviewed -*
*I have dementia... I don't remember -*
*it's hard to give an answer about the part of life*
*based on all the things you don't remember.*

*I like to talk about what's in front..*
*I vaguely*
*remember*
*feeling churned up by these questions*
*probing*
*digging*
*about Ruth*
*about my feelings*
*and guilt.*

*Asking me the deepest darkest secrets-*
*but really it's not a secret,*
*its my life,*
*but because I don't remember my life,*
*it seems alien*
*and strange to search for answers.*

*And we*
*speak of*
*so much -*

*information -*
*emotion -*
*fear -*
*trying to be brave*
*and honest.*

*Yes, I really wanted to be honest about what this life is like-*
*but the shape of the questions don't enable me to*
*be honest in the way I wished.*
*Square bricks in triangle spaces.*

*After two days of*
*talking talking talking*
*email - faxes- scans- modern technology-*
*the photographer came*
*and a make-up lady*
*and a stylist.*
*It should be fun -*
*new clothes*
*new style*
*keeping the 'me'-ness of me?*

*But no talk*
*or niceties*
*just layers of foundation*
*blusher*
*lipstick*
*fake lashes*
*plucked brows*
*high arches*
*tights*

to hold up dreads
ethnic top
colours
no glasses
and them amongst themselves
doing their job
and us arms out... being dressed
and fussed and polished.

They told us we were perfect-
taking pictures
snap snap
heads in frame
and smile.

Finally
the finished product -
black print on glossy paper.
Headline 'The Real Still Alice'
and my story staring back at me -
a sense of unreality
and sadness for Ruth.
It's factual about me -
they reached their conclusion
fairly -
previous paranoia and panicking
recedes -
maybe it was unfounded -
yes - its all correct
a reasonable reflection

*but just words -*
*and my reality means*
*I read the article and feel nothing*
*but perhaps if it helps the public-*
*the people out there,*
*then I am pleased.*

*On my lap is the magazine*
*and a photograph is*
*centre-page -*
*Ruth's arms around my neck -*
*mother and daughter -*
*portrayed with perfection -*
*glossy lips*
*smiling*
*towards*
*our*
*'Fabulous'*
*invisible*
*Sunday afternoon*
*audience.*

*But I see myself*
*and think*
*"Who is she?"*

## Snippet 5

You
look down from death
and I am looking back.

Do my ancestors long gone
whisper
about preciousness of life
and the sanctity
of being alive?

Am I doing the best of
helping  those around me to be happy?

Am I making the most of my
small short journey?

## Snippet 6

We are the only beings on this planet and possibly the universe
that create the need for stuff...

## Snippet 7

*We are prolific consumers*
*but at any cost?*

*No bee: no honey*
*no honey: no money*
*no bee: no flower*
*no flower: no power.*

## Snippet 8

*We have a duty to our planet to only make things that can be*
*recycled time and time again.*
*Manufactures should only make the* **one** *that can be*
*reused*
*because nature would do that..it would only make the* **one**
*that can be reused - because we are the only creatures*
*that make entire mountains and islands*
*out of waste.*

# Walking on the Clouds

One thousand one hundred and twenty-two miles
to the south
As the crow flies
from my bed in Hanwell
and twenty two hours in a car.
My husband and my daughter
and me
crossing countries
reaching the top edge of Spain
by breakfast time
watching the landscape change from Basque
to Cordoba
rainy-green pasture full of swaying cows
with rich milky udders.
Peace rapidly baptised into the mayhem of Madrid -
five lanes of traffic -
wits - scared out of -
driving on wrong side of road -
tired eyes navigating the tangle
of tarmac and steel.
A day later arriving in Granada -
loose in the cosmopolitan vibe
Moors and Christians -
death and fire and lust
etched into the walls of Alhambra,
knee-deep in history -
a place of education
of art and culture
and us pausing for breath

before the road to Baza
and huge lakes and spas
an environment to fall in love with -
hot and dry
and us to stay
three months
absorbing the novelty,
whilst eyes out and the search for a home
amid cave houses
built into the rock of the mountains
skewered into the landscape like ticks.
Hundreds of years
of light and bright and airy living -
cool in the summer
and warm in the winter.
But temptation aside
above us we spy
a mountain
'Los Filabres'
clothed with
five villages winding
their way down -
beautiful
easy reach
of lakes
and skiing and
the desert beyond.
Benitagla - third village down.
A seventeen mile twirl
from the top
to bottom.

And there in the clouds
a shack
with a good roof and 'potential'.
Three tiny windows - no design for glass -
wire mesh to keep the bugs out,
a tiny heavy door
and in the porch a little hatch
for the key
and a chunk of wood
to push to open.
An old farm building
once full of steaming
livestock -
with a pig trough in Ruth's bedroom.
Tile floors,
straw walls
and centuries of withered old faces
peeping through the cracks
watching us move in.

In the beginning we
make windows
and the very first Ruth and I put in together.
We don't have beds
but we have cool ground
and it had been a dwelling to others before us
albeit rustic and ramshackle.
The former occupants
were proud that they had left us
a Formica table

and a leather settee
a fridge and
an old old cooker that caught fire,
a sink
and hot and cold taps,
a bath and a toilet.
It was only after we bought it -
we realised there was only cold water
no pipes
no boiler
no plumbing.
so for us
tin baths
and unsullied cool water.
But we felt earthy
and alive
and ran to meet the
tooting bread van at 12.30 each day.
It took a long time to make friends -
they were suspicious.
It was a property boom
and of course the natives were
pleased to get money from the houses -
but they wondered what the hell we doing there -
we unsettled their set-in ways.
They seemed untouched by the evolving world-
woman wearing aprons and skirts
living off the land,
a donkey to fetch and carry -
hay for mattresses and

a once-a-week mini-van
selling lentils, flour, basics... no baked beans
or spaghetti hoops for our English bellies.
And no internet or telephone
for a hello.
Paella for celebration
and a very recent goodbye to fascism
Franco's old soldiers
still smoking pipes in the village below
and a mayor that wouldn't
acknowledge us.

After my husband
left me
or me him
I found it easier
to focus on
what I should
be doing.
Ten years pass
sorting
working
painting
decorating
gardening.
Ruth grew into
a teenager
and I grew ill.
They couldn't understand me
on that hill top in Spain -

They thought I was a druggie
or putting it on.
My teeth fell out -
I became a skeleton -
I had strokes and my abilities
vanished.
When they realised -
they gave me biscuits
and Ruth, treats
but by and by
I had to leave.

More years pass
I live with my parents
In England
awaiting diagnosis.
My mind in hibernation.

But the day comes
And Wow
I'm home
back in the clouds -
welcomed by neighbours -
men and woman
a kiss and another -
its infinite space
the air is pure.

Here
I feel a different Jacqui -

the pace of life lets you be slow,
we are no longer isolated.
It's very social -
walk into the bar
be given a glass of wine -
its a Euro.

Here
it's easy to be giving.

Men sit in a row outside the taverna
on little chairs
as the sun dips -
drinking tiny glasses of wine and
woman gather in the square
under the acacia tree...
every evening
the same as the evening before
and you drift backwards
into timeless centuries.

I go back because I have to
but
I never want to leave.

I only leave
because
these days
I have a plane ticket.

# Nature and Philosophy

I love everything about nature
Its diversity, its colour, its sound
and always find myself stunned by
how a tiny insect to a huge mammal
can adapt.
The insect can change colour or appearance to guard
and protect itself-
the caterpillar can grow wings,
the fish can grow legs,
the fox can become urban.

We are so dazzled by the array of
colour within the animal kingdom -
That without spiders and birds and butterflies
giraffes and tigers and sheep
we would have no inspiration as humans-
because we could never make those shades up-
not in our dreams.

We have wars...
humans have wars
but insects and animals
protect themselves individually
or in groups
they know they have the human as an enemy,
whatever species they are -
but they also know their
enemy in the animal kingdom.

If you are an impala
you run from a lion
if you are a rabbit
you run from the fox
all creatures' instincts are geared to flee
their enemies.

From flowers -
to butterflies - to birds -
science creates
an awareness of diversity in every form.
Inquisitive enquiry and wonder -
but quiet the hunger for more
and be content to immerse
body and soul in the rhythm
of our human cycle.

Don't try to interfere
or manufacture longer life.
Do not suspend your death in
formaldehyde
awaiting restoration

Find Inspiration in discovery.
Develop
ideals that aid us - through observing nature.
We have all we need here to teach us-
Animals have adapted to changing
climate
and deforestation.

The mud frog
buries himself in damp earth -
he knows his purpose -
he does his purpose,
nature is looking for nothing
more than survival
within the constraints that it is given.

A deer isn't going to walk into the front room
and want to watch Coronation Street-
it ain't gonna happen -
but we walk into a deer's environment and think
"mmmm delicious stew"
or
"Nice set of antlers to be mounted on my wall".

Each year we find new species
that we have never realised -
Beings that can survive in complete darkness
a thousand leagues under the sea
or a bloom in a barren burning desert
that lives for  months on its own moisture.
Humans rely on outside forces
gifted by nature -
gas and electric,
coal and oil,
wind and sea.

If you take away these things
people would not know
how to survive.

From the beginning there has been a natural cycle...
the buzzard eats the mouse
the mouse harvests the corn
the bee pollinates the flower
the flower photosynthesises.

Da Vinci first designed the helicopter
and that was inspired by nature -
the sycamore seed pod
spinning to earth in the spring.

And if the birds hadn't been here
we would never
have thought about flying.

When we make something it always
seems to cause damage
to the sea,
the rivers,
the countryside,
the ice fields -
we don't see the consequences of our actions
we only desire the results.
We just don't realise how much we need nature to keep us safe
and she has provided us with all the answers.

If only we could open our eyes -
we don't need to fabricate.
We poison ourselves and allow commerce to control our thoughts -
we are brainwashed into thinking we
must must must consume no matter the cost.

We suck the planet dry of resources
and then drill holes looking for more.
We are insatiable -
but if you accept that our planet is a living thing-
why would you want to take the contents of its belly
and pollute the air it breathes.

I used to have a dream when I was a kid
that a special army would come and put special
dust on everyone and everyone would be asleep for a week
and while everyone is asleep...
everything would be put back the way it should be -
all bad plastics would be gone...
new trees would line the streets,
the paths would be lined with flowers,
all the things we needed would be there
nature would be abundant.
We would have cars and houses-
but the unnecessary things would be gone.

There would be no need for consumerism...
things would be basics...
there is enough for everyone.

We swapsie what we have between countries and continents
and so it carries on until there aren't any swapsies left
and then we are allowed to make things
but only good things
we are allowed to advance technology but only if it does good
and doesn't create waste or poison.

If you need a new telly
you can buy a new telly
but you can't throw yours out...
you have to give it to someone else.

We have so many alternatives,
Through science-
through knowledge-
through education
even street kids in Africa know how to
make light bulbs out of Coca-Cola bottles.

All the answers are here
on the earth -
without this smog and suffocation
and destruction.

We can regenerate using the attributes of nature
and learn to be satisfied
with being a part of the natural cycle of life -
We don't get more colourful
There isn't any more.
Life is what it is.
It has a beginning,
a middle and an end.

**Gratitude.**

**Jacqui Peedell** (left)
and **Jo Davies** (right)